D1622099

50

Ways to Add
Energy, Enthusiasm
& Enjoyment
to Your Life

Julie Alexander

50

Ways to Add
Energy, Enthusiasm
& Enjoyment
to Your Life

Julie Alexander

Printed in the United State of America.

Cover design and text layout by Ad Graphics,
Tulsa, Oklahoma.

Library of Congress Catalog Number: 97-093958

ISBN: 0-9659310-0-5

Published by:

Great Days Press
a subsidiary of Great Days Presentations
2002 Shari Lane
Garland, TX 75043

Order Information.
To order more copies of this book or to
receive information on programs
or other products by
Julie Alexander, contact:
Great Days Presentations
by calling:

(972) 240-5717

A little help from my friends...

Special thanks to:

Barb and Jim Weems at Ad Graphics, Tulsa, OK for being so easy to work with and such "pros."

Lou Beth Birdwell, Sue Dance, Kathleen Fawcett, and Lonnie Hitchcock for their sharp eyes and pencils.

My colleagues in the National Speakers Association and the North Texas Speakers Association for providing the encouragement and the expertise to help me get started.

My family who supported me and encouraged me all the way.

Dedication
To my family.

This book is for:

My dad, who made every day a great one.

My mother, who is my best friend and biggest fan.

My sons, Adam and Ben, who have added humor and joy to my life, encouraged me, and provided me with great material.

My daughter-in-law, Amber, who is a special friend.

My husband, Ken, who believes in me even when I don't believe in myself and who makes every day fun.

Contents

Introduction

I believe that happiness is a decision and that, even in the worst of times, we have the ability to make a conscious choice regarding our response. We can determine to make the best of our situation, to learn and to grow from it, and to move beyond it.

One of the first quotations in this book reads, "How we spend our days is how we spend our lives." In truth, our lives are nothing more than the culmination of our days, so if we live each day to its fullest – seeking knowledge, health, joy, wisdom, fulfilling relationships, peace, purpose – the end result will be a life which is full, rewarding, and enjoyable.

If we could make every day a great day, it stands to reason that we'd have a great life. So the purpose of this little book is to share a few ideas regarding some of the things we *can* do to create great days for ourselves and for those around us. Maybe it will serve as a reminder that we are to use the time we've been given to become productive, purposeful human beings.

I hope that you'll find the thoughts in this book helpful. I hope, too, that this collection of stories, wit, and wisdom will make you smile, make you think, and touch your heart. It's not rocket science. But it is a heart-felt expression of my personal thoughts regarding living each day to the fullest and finding joy, fun, peace, and purpose in this precious gift of life.

Wishing you great days,

Julie Alexander

About the author...

Julie Alexander is a dynamic, versatile professional speaker, author, and corporate educator. Her warm, down-to-earth style, as well as her wit, wisdom, and thorough research, allows her to "connect" with her audiences in a positive way. Julie provides groups of all kinds with motivational, content-based programs focused on creating positive workplaces and successful lives.

A resident of the Dallas area, Julie is a graduate of Texas Christian University and holds a master's degree from Southern Methodist University. Her background includes experience in business, teaching, and television.

Julie is an active member of the National Speakers Association and is past president of the North Texas Speakers Association. In her personal life, she is married and is the mother of two sons.

If you'd like to have Julie speak to your organization, contact her at Great Days Presentations (972) 240-5717.

Great Days

1
Make the Most of Today.

"This is the day the Lord has made.
Let us rejoice and be glad in it."
Psalm 118:24

"Dying is less sad than having lived too little."
Gloria Steinem

"How we spend our days is how
we spend our lives."
Annie Dillard

D o you know anyone who is so pre-occupied with the past or so focused on the future that they miss the joy of today? That probably could be said of all of us at one time or another. For some, the "good old days" of the past or the "great expectations" of the future hold more interest or delight than the present. For others, past mistakes or tragedies or concerns about what might happen in the future keep them from any enjoyment or pleasure that the current moment might provide.

Those people who spend their lives searching for that elusive state that we call happiness tend to be the ones who don't recognize the pleasures of the "now." They fail to realize that perhaps real contentment comes from the simple things...having a quiet lunch with one's best friend, walking in the woods, enjoying the company of a child, curling up with a good book – simply recognizing the pleasures of the moment.

Those who experience the greatest joy in life are those who make the most of *today* – the *now*, the only part of life over which we have any control. Alice Roosevelt Longworth, daughter of Theodore Roosevelt, was known for her sharp wit and her acid tongue, but she also had a great zest for living. When Alice was in her nineties, Lady Bird Johnson described her as "undaunted by old age, bristling with the quality of aliveness," and when asked if she was nostalgic, Alice replied, "Certainly not. What could be more interesting than today?"

MCI ran a television commercial recently which said, "Is this a great time or what?" This *is* a great time. Despite the negative elements which exist in our world, it's a fascinating time, especially for those who make the most of today, those who really *live*.

Iphigene Ochs, whose father founded *The New York Times*, was another dynamic woman who lived life to its fullest. On her eightieth birthday, her granddaughter wrote to her in a birthday greeting, "You're a human *living*, not just a human being." What a tribute!

Many of us spend our lives just *being*, shuffling from one day to the next, not taking advantage of today. Sadly, those who live like that wake up one day to discover that life has passed them by, and there is no turning back. Perhaps our philosophy should be to look to the future, learn from the past, and live today.

Remember ~ "How we spend our days is how we spend our lives," so make the most of *today*. Enjoy the moment; appreciate the present; relish the *now*.

2

Learn Something.

*"If you think education is expensive,
try ignorance."*
Derek Bok

*"I will study and prepare myself, and then
someday my chance will come."*
Abraham Lincoln

*"If you feed your mind as often as you feed your
stomach, then you'll never have to worry about
feeding your stomach or a roof over your head
or clothes on your back."*
Albert Einstein

*"Education is a wonderful thing. If you couldn't
sign your name, you'd have to pay cash."*
Rita Mae Brown

*"Every man is ignorant –
just on different subjects."*
Will Rogers

We've all heard the phrase "live and learn," but why not "learn...and live"! Learning opens up our minds and imaginations to new concepts and ideas. It keeps us from being bored...and boring.

One of the best things that we can do for ourselves is to remember that school is never out. Continuing to learn new information and to try new things can make our days challenging and rewarding. There's so much to know, so much to see, so many things to read, so many places to go, and pushing ourselves to learn makes life more interesting and exciting.

In May, 1997, Mary Fasano graduated from Harvard University. You may be saying, "So what? Lots of people graduate from college." But what made Mary's accomplishment so special was that she was 89 years old. Family circumstances forced Mary to leave school in the eighth grade, but she was determined to get an education. Mary said, "I made a vow to myself that no matter how old I was, I would go back to school. It never left me. Never left me."

But a lifetime of work and family delayed her dream. While working as a weaver, she met her future husband. They married, and in the following years, she became the mother of four, the grandmother of 20, and the great-grandmother of 18. In 1979, Mary graduated from high school...at age 71. Her college degree wasn't an easy accomplishment. It took 17 years, one evening class at a time, and required a 45-minute commute on the subway which departed the campus at 9:30 or 10:00 o'clock at night.

Was it worth the effort? Mary Fasano says, "Yes!" Mary credits her continuing education to staving off the senility that has put her two surviving sisters in nursing homes. Her advice to other senior citizen students is clear, "Don't stop – keep going. It will be worth it in the end. To have knowledge is to have power."

When my mother was 81 years old, she called one morning to tell me about an article she'd read in the newspaper. The article was about a woman who, at 96, was very bright and mentally alert. When asked how she had continued to stay so sharp, the woman answered that she tried to learn something new every day. My mother said, "I think that's a good idea, and I wanted to call and tell you that I've learned something new today." This was during the time of the Gulf War, and my mother said, "Today I learned how to spell Norman Schwarzkopf, and I wanted to call and tell you before I forgot!" At age 81, my mother was sharpening her skills and pushing herself to learn and to grow. It's never too late, is it? School is never out, and being a perpetual student can add energy, enthusiasm, and enjoyment to life.

What about you? What have you learned today? Ignorance is not bliss. It's poverty, depression, dullness, boredom. Learn something today. Learn...and live!

3

Say "I Love You."

"Shower the people you love with love,
Show them the way that you feel;
Everything will be much better if you only will."
James Taylor

"I just called to say 'I love you.'"
Stevie Wonder

"All you need is love. Love is all you need."
The Beatles

Who do you love? Stop reading right now, and make a list of all the people that you love – your spouse, your children, your grandchildren, siblings, parents, neighbors, special friends, relatives, colleagues at work, church friends – even your pets.

I *love...*

_____ _____

_____ _____

_____ _____

_____ _____

_____   _____

_____   _____

_____   _____

_____   _____

_____   _____

_____   _____

_____   _____

_____   _____

_____   _____

_____   _____

_____   _____

_____   _____

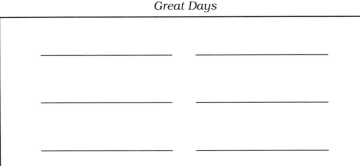

I hope the list is a long one, because the more we love others, the more we are loved.

After you've made the list, start at the top and begin to tell these people how much you care about them. Said sincerely and meaningfully, those three little words are the sweetest anyone can hear.

We get so busy that we don't stop and tell people how much they mean to us, what they've done for us, how important they are in our lives. As the song says, "Have I told you lately that I love you?" In most relationships, the answer to that question is probably, "No, you haven't." We get so busy that we forget to tell people how much we care. It takes a little time, and for some of us, it takes overcoming our hesitancy to share our feelings, but it can mean so much and can do so much to strengthen relationships.

There are many people who have a hard time saying, "I love you." The feelings are there, but they just can't verbalize those feelings. Usually those people are the ones who didn't hear "I love you" too often when they were growing up. For most, it wasn't that they weren't loved, but many families – even loving, supportive ones – don't always say the words. A husband, for example, doesn't always tell his wife that he loves her. He assumes that she already knows it, so why mention it? After all, he works hard for her, provides her with a home, food, clothing, all the necessities and the niceties of life. She should know by his actions how he feels. Why be redundant and tell her in words?

Parents, particularly those with pre-teens and teenagers, often stop telling their children, "I love you." (For one thing, children at that age sometimes can be pretty unlovable!) But, also, after the first few times the child reacts negatively to being told that he or she is loved, the parents get the message and stop saying it...and sadly, may never say it again. And yet, teenagers need the constant assurance that they are loved. Pick your time to tell them. Don't do it in public or in front of their friends, but quietly, sincerely, privately, and often say, "I love you." Now, don't be disappointed. Don't expect them to throw their arms around you and profess their deep love for you! That probably won't happen. But tell your teenagers, "I love you." They need and want to hear it whether they admit it or not.

Tell your parents, your grandparents, your in-laws, your aunts and uncles, "I love you." We never outgrow the need to know that we are loved.

My husband's parents had a hard time verbalizing their feelings. We knew that they loved us, but they never said it. In their later years, my husband and I started ending our visits both in person and on the phone with "I love you." The first few times we did this, the response was total silence, as if they really didn't know what to think, let alone what to say. As time went on, when we said, "I love you," my father-in-law would say, "Yep," which we decided was his way of saying, "I love you, too." But my mother-in-law just couldn't respond. She was a woman who desperately needed love and attention but had a hard time giving love and attention to others. However, one day shortly before she died, I was leaving her hospital room, and I said, "Helen, I love you." And she replied, "I love you, too, Julie Margaret" (which was the name she always called me). It was the first, and the last, time she said it to me, but I'll never forget it.

Powerful words, memorable words, magic words. Say, "I love you," and expect miracles.

4

Have a Positive Attitude.

*"Most folks are just about as happy as they
make up their minds to be."*
Abraham Lincoln

*"Any fact facing us is not as important as our
attitude toward it, for that determines our
success or failure."*
Dr. Norman Vincent Peale

*"Keep your face to the sunshine, and you
cannot see the shadows."*
Helen Keller

*"Happiness and misery depend as much on
temperament as on fortune."*
La Rochefoucauld

*"Whether you think you can or think you can't,
you're right."*
Henry Ford

*"The last of human freedoms – to choose one's
attitude in any given set of circumstances,
to choose one's own way."*
Viktor Frankl

A braham Lincoln certainly knew what
he was talking about, didn't he?
Wouldn't you agree that most folks

really are just about as happy as they make up their minds to be? Happiness is, indeed, a decision.

All of us have known people who've suffered unbelievable tragedies in their lives. They've endured the tragic death or illness of spouses, children, parents. They've suffered physical and emotional pain. They've lost all their worldly possessions to flood or fire, natural or financial disaster. And yet many of those people have just decided that they're not going to be defeated by those events. They've decided that they're going to be happy no matter what and to make the most of their difficult situations by having a positive attitude. Dr. David G. Myers, who has spent years researching this elusive thing called "happiness" says, "...well-being is a state of mind...our happiness depends less on our objective circumstances than on how we respond to them."

I didn't even know what "attitude" was until I was in the 7th grade. My English teacher, Miss Petway, was a rather eccentric woman who tried to, but rarely did, control our class. The boy who sat in front of me seemed to delight in provoking her in typical seventh-grade style. One of her frequent statements to him was, "Charles! Charles! I don't like your attitude." In other words, Miss Petway didn't like Charles' disposition and the manner in which he showed it.

Our attitude is our disposition, our response to a situation or condition, and although we can't always control the circumstances of our lives, we can control our attitudes. As we've often heard, it isn't so much what happens to us but how we choose to respond to those events that makes the difference.

In aeronautics, the word "attitude" refers to the orientation of an aircraft's axes relative to some reference line or plane, such as the horizon. To put it in simpler terms, attitude is the angle between the airplane and the ground. The pilot controls the attitude of the plane, and we control our attitude.

To have great days, realize that no matter what happens – whether you're faced with a major tragedy or the trivial irritations that life can sometimes dish out – you can control how you respond. If you make the decision to deal with all the events of your life – big or small, traumatic or trivial, devastating or disappointing – in a positive way, you'll be much happier and much stronger emotionally. As the Apostle Paul wrote, "Be joyful always; pray continually; give thanks in all circumstances."

Someone has said that pain is inevitable, but suffering is optional. How true that is. Decide that you're going to be joyful in all situations. You'll feel more in control of your circumstances, rather than feeling that your circumstances are controlling you. You'll feel that you have your hands on the steering wheel of your life. You'll be able to say to yourself, "I may not like the things which have happened to me, but I'm making up my mind to deal with them in a positive way." And you and everyone you encounter will like your attitude.

5
Look Good.

"Clothes make the man."
William Shakespeare

"I base my fashion taste on what doesn't itch."
Gilda Radner

*"Genius is of small use to a woman who does
not know how to do her hair."*
Edith Wharton

*"It now takes me twice as long to look half
as good as I used to."*
Unknown

*"All God's children are not beautiful. Most of
God's children are, in fact, barely presentable."*
Fran Lebowitz

*"Taking care of one's hair requires so much time
and energy; I think it makes us irritable."*
Alva Vanderbilt

"Women must suffer to be beautiful."
Lonnie Hitchcock

You've had this happen, haven't you? It's Saturday or one of those days that you don't have any place in particular that you have to go. You decide to stay at home to cook or to clean or to do yard work. You get up, throw on a pair of old jeans or shorts, put on a T-shirt and get busy. But after a time, you realize that you need just one or two items from the grocery store or the hardware store. You certainly don't want to have to go through the entire procedure of taking a shower, doing your hair, getting dressed...you know, the "make-yourself-presentable" routine. So you decide to live dangerously. You get in the car and go on your errands as you are. And it never fails. Don't you usually see someone you know? And isn't it often someone whom you haven't seen in five years and probably won't see again for five more? You can imagine them telling their friends about seeing you and how terrible you looked. Why is it that when you've got on a new outfit and are looking pretty good, you don't see anyone you know? It's a law of the universe.

Now, I'm a great believer in having some days when you don't dress up. In my business, I have to put on the dreaded pantyhose and heels just about every day, so I delight in those days when I can abandon make-up and wear my old clothes and tennis shoes.

But if you're in the dumps or having a bad day, it may be a good idea to shape up your appearance. Maybe you've noticed that when you're down, if you'll take a shower, wash your hair, put on your make-up, brush your teeth, and put on fresh, clean clothes, you feel better. Research tells us that children tend to behave better in school and perform better on tests when they are dressed nicely and are well-groomed.

Perhaps there's a lesson here for all of us. Look sharp, and you'll feel sharp. Having a bad day? Do something to make yourself look and feel more attractive. You'll have a better day. Do it to lift your spirits...and as a courtesy to those who have to look at you!

6

Take Care of Yourself.

*"If I'd known I was going to live this long, I
would have taken better care of myself."*
Unknown

*"I could never have an affair. I don't have the
energy or the underwear for it."*
Erma Bombeck

We've all heard it said that if you don't have your health, you don't have anything. If you don't believe that, just ask those who've experienced illness or problems with their health, and they'll confirm that this old adage is certainly true. Certainly, one of the best things you can do to insure "great days" is to take care of yourself.

In the mid-1970s, we had an energy crisis in this country. We could buy gasoline only on certain days of the week. We were advised to limit the use of fuel and electrical power because we were running out of these resources. Back then, I stopped using my electric can opener in an effort to conserve electricity!

Although the energy crisis that loomed large in the mid-70s no longer seems to be of great concern, I'm convinced that there is an energy crisis in this country, but it has little to do with petroleum. The real energy crisis is a *personal* energy crisis.

We're tired. We don't get enough rest. We don't eat right. We don't take care of ourselves, and we're suffering as a result of it.

You've all heard the flight attendants go through their spiel on the safety features of the airplane and what to do in case of an emergency. In the early phase of each flight, the attendant reminds passengers that in the unlikely event of a loss of cabin pressure, an oxygen mask will drop from the ceiling. You are instructed to pull the tubing to the full extent, place the mask over your nose and mouth, and breath normally. (By the way, if you've ever been in this situation, it is impossible to breath normally!)

Then they add that if you're traveling with a small child or someone who needs assistance, you're to place the mask on yourself *first* and then assist the other person.

There's a lesson here. We can't possibly take care of anyone else – our children, our spouse, our parents, our relatives, our neighbors, our friends, our business or community obligations – unless we take care of ourselves first.

To have lots of great days, eat right, exercise, rest...take care of yourself.

7

Celebrate!

"Drink champagne for defeats as well as for victories. It tastes the same, and you need it more."
Unknown

"Don't wait to celebrate!"
Julie Alexander

I love parties, don't you? I love holidays and birthdays and special occasions. But I think that we need to create lots of reasons to celebrate and not save celebrating just for the big events. Celebrating many things – the big things, the little things, the important things, the insignificant things – makes life fun.

It's important to take time to celebrate even the smallest accomplishments or the ordinary events. When our children were growing up, we'd go out to dinner to celebrate report cards. (That was my idea. Pretty clever, huh?) Our boys didn't have to make all "A's" for us to celebrate and to congratulate. We'd sometimes celebrate the survival of a particularly challenging class, the completion of a project, a small victory, or lessons learned from a defeat. We made banners to welcome the boys home from camp or Dad home from a business trip. For birthday breakfasts, we even put candles in bowls of Cheerios!

One of my favorite people in the world was my Aunt Hattie. She was my mother's youngest sister and a unique individual – bright, charming, interesting, funny, a lady far ahead of her time.

Hattie never married. She was a career woman in the days when that in itself was unique. A petite redhead, she had a dynamic personality and always loved a party. She was a world traveler, a voracious reader, and a fiercely competitive bridge player. She was a natural poet who delighted friends and family with her "odes" for special occasions. She spoke fluent Spanish, a little French, and had a contagious laugh that seemed to come from the bottoms of her feet and fill her entire being.

When Aunt Hattie died in 1982, my mother and her sister had the task of going through Hattie's personal belongings. In the process, they found an envelope. Inside was a considerable amount of cash along with some instructions. They were to take the money and have a party, a celebration in her honor. There was also a little poem, written for a special occasion. It read:

"When I am gone, do not be sad;
Think about the fun we had;
Think about the laughs we shared
And laugh again."

And that's what we did. A small group of Hattie's family members and friends enjoyed a lovely brunch at a fine restaurant in her honor. We tried not to be sad. We thought about the laughs we'd shared...and laughed again.

Celebrate *something* today. Celebrations don't have to be big, flashy, or expensive to be fun. And the reasons to celebrate don't have to be limited to national or religious holidays or milestone events. In fact, don't wait to celebrate. Celebrate because it's Tuesday...or because it's sunny or snowing or windy. Celebrate that the sun came up, that the car started, that the lights came on when you flipped the switch. Celebrate that you have a friend. Celebrate the dog's birthday, your parents' anniversary, National Lawn Sprinkler Month. Celebrate that you can read, that you could get out of bed this morning, that you are loved.

Send a card, make a cake, give a balloon, wear a party hat, open the champagne, go to dinner, light a candle, put up a banner – celebrate life! And have a great day.

8

Develop Positive Partnerships.

"The nice thing about teamwork is that you always have others on your side."
Margaret Carty

"No one succeeds alone."
Ray Kroc

"It's so much more friendly with two."
Winnie the Pooh

In 1624 the poet John Donne wrote, "No man is an island." How true it is. We human beings are interdependent. We need each other.

Those people who seem to have the most great days are those who have many positive partnerships. In a partnership, each person brings something to the relationship, and the result is greater than the sum of the parts. Lady Bird Johnson said of her partnership with her husband, "We were better together than we were apart. He made me grow. He flattered me, shoved me, ridiculed me, loved me into doing things I never thought I was big enough to do."

Think about all the positive partners you have in your life. There are, of course, the obvious ones – partnerships with your spouse, children, siblings, customers, friends, business associates – but what about the partnerships you have with your doctor, your mechanic, your insurance agent, your clergy, your hair stylist. What about the person at the dry cleaners,the grocery store checker, your pharmacist...the list goes on and on.

We have endless opportunities to develop positive partnerships with people we encounter each day. Think of how you benefit from association with your partners. How do they benefit from their association with you?

Make a list of your positive partners. If they work behind the counter at the dry cleaners or sack your groceries, you may not have given them much thought. But starting today, learn their names. Find out something about them. Get to know them as individuals, and recognize them as partners – not just nameless faces. See them not just in terms of what they do for you but as friends, colleagues, partners, and think about what you can do for them. If you begin thinking of these people as "partners" rather than just acquaintances, you'll have a different attitude toward them.

Those people who enjoy a supportive network of family and friends tend to be happier, healthier, more productive, and they enjoy life more fully. Having positive partners can help us cope with the bad times and relish the good ones. We certainly need our positive partners during the tough times. But wouldn't you agree that in times of joy, it is more joyful when we have someone with whom to share it?

Are you a "positive partner"? Are you bringing your best to each relationship? In a partnership there has to be a willingness to give and take. There are times when one needs to be supportive and others when one needs supporting. There are times when one must encourage and times when one needs encouragement. Be willing to reach out your hand and help when your partners are struggling, because the day will come when you'll need a hand to hold, a hand to pull you up – the steady, firm hand of your positive partner.

9

Laugh at Yourself.

*"Blessed are those who can laugh
at themselves, for they will never
cease to be amused."*
Unknown

*"One out of four people in this country
is mentally unbalanced. Think of your three
closest friends ~ if they seem okay,
than you're the one."*
Ann Landers

*"Angels fly because they take
themselves lightly."*
G.K. Chesterton

"Laughter is inner jogging."
Norman Cousins

A reporter once asked Bess Truman, wife of the 33rd President of the United States, what characteristics she thought were the most important for the wife of a President to have, and Bess replied, "Good health, and a well-developed sense of humor." She was certainly right about that. Those characteristics are important not just for First Ladies but for all of us.

If we want to have great days, we have to be able to laugh at ourselves and to not take ourselves too seriously. Some of our best laughs should be the result of our laughing at ourselves, of finding humor in our mistakes or our shortcomings.

On the Riverwalk in San Antonio, Texas, there's a restaurant called "Dick's Last Resort." Like many of the Riverwalk restaurants, Dick's has outdoor tables and is a great spot for watching the tourists stroll along the river. One day my husband and I were walking in front of that restaurant when I saw a quarter on the crowded sidewalk. Not being one to pass up money, I bent down to pick it up. But the quarter wouldn't budge. No matter what I did, the quarter refused to be picked up. To my surprise, and to the amusement of the outdoor diners at Dick's, it was glued to the sidewalk, placed there by the management as part of the entertainment for the customers. Was I embarrassed! Now, I could have gotten mad and upset and could have allowed being the brunt of the joke to put me in a bad mood. But the better reaction was to laugh right along with the patrons at Dick's and enjoy the moment.

When I was about twelve years old, my family and I were invited to Sue Ming's wedding. Sue had grown up in our neighborhood, but we had moved away several years before and had not seen her or her parents, Morris and Elaine, in some time. We were excited about attending this celebration as it would be a good opportunity not only to visit with them but also to see other friends from the old neighborhood.

The night of the wedding we were running late and left the house without the invitation, but my dad said he knew where the church was and exactly how to get there. Sure enough we arrived and got seated just minutes before the wedding party was to start down the aisle. As we settled into our seats, my mother leaned over to me and said, "I think the organist is Morris' brother. I know he's a musician, and that man looks just like him." I agreed. He was, as we say in Texas, a "spittin' image" of Mr. Ming.

The groom's family was seated, and then the mother of the bride came down the aisle. Since we'd arrived late, we were seated over to one side and couldn't see too well, but as she passed by, my mother whispered, "Elaine has lost weight. She looks so slim."

My mother was looking around the church, trying to spot familiar faces. "I'm so glad we came," she whispered again. "I don't see anyone else from the old neighborhood."

After the bridesmaids and the groomsmen had taken their places, the anticipated moment arrived, the time for the bride and her father to come down the aisle. As the congregation stood and turned to watch the grand entrance, my parents and I had quite a surprise. The bride was not Sue Ming! Both the bride and the father of the bride were total strangers.

At that point my parents and I began to attempt to control the overwhelming laughter that was building up inside. (Have you ever noticed that things are so much funnier when you're in a place where you're not supposed to laugh!) Of course what made it so amusing was remembering my mother's comments preceding our discovery.

It took every ounce of willpower and self-control we possessed to get us through that ceremony. We'd made a mistake, but the only thing to do was to laugh at ourselves.

Often it's the little things in life that cause us the most frustration and also provide the best opportunities to find humor in every day life. Have you ever misplaced something? It's so frustrating not to be able to find something that you know you have! Recently, I couldn't find the grated parmesan cheese. I knew I had some, because I'd just used it the day before. I looked everywhere – in the pantry, in the refrigerator, in every storage cabinet. Finally, I just gave up and announced to my family that they'd have to eat their spaghetti without the parmesan cheese. That night when I was cleaning up the kitchen after dinner, I found the parmesan cheese...under the kitchen sink! Well, it was in a green container. Guess I thought it was a can of Comet cleanser!

When things go wrong today...and they may...try to find a way to laugh at yourself. Laugh at your mistakes. Laugh at your short-comings. Laugh at the fact that you don't know everything and that you don't always do things right. As some wise person said, "If you can look in the mirror without laughing, you have no sense of humor."

Here's an extra benefit of laughter – William Fry, MD, an emeritus associate clinical professor at Stanford University School of Medicine, says that laughing 100 times is equivalent to a 15-minute stationary bike workout! Which would you choose?

Laugh at yourself...and have a great day!

10

Listen to Music.

"Music is well said to be the speech of angels."
Thomas Carlyle

*"I don't know anything about music,
but I know what I like."*
Sir Max Beerbohm

"I like that old time rock and roll."
Bob Seger

Music surely must have almost magical powers. I'm sure you've had the experience of hearing a song that you haven't heard in years, and yet you find you can remember every word. No doubt, you have heard a song that immediately brought back vivid memories of a certain time, a particular place, a special person. Music locks itself into our brains and never seems to let go, and it can have a positive or a negative effect on our moods. It has the ability to lift our spirits or to make us melancholy.

What kind of music do you like? I like a variety. If you were to get into my car and check the radio stations, you'd find that they range from pop to classical and from country to jazz. I like gospel, blues, opera, choral, rock and roll, and everything in between.

If I am really stressed or have a lot on my mind, I turn on the classics. For me, classical music has a calming effect and yet the ability, too, to stimulate creativity. Sometimes I'm in the mood for luscious love songs. Other times the lyrics and the beat of a country song or the energy of the "golden oldies" of rock and roll can rev me up and get me going. Research studies have shown that workers who are allowed to listen to music tend to be more productive and have a higher level of morale, especially if they get to choose the music.

Find out what kind of music makes you feel good, and turn it on. It can alter your attitude.

If you should see me driving down the road, I'll probably be listening to and singing along with my favorite music of the moment. I may be conducting an orchestra while listening to a symphony or snapping my fingers and movin' with the beat of a rock and roll favorite. (Much to my family's dismay, I've given up all pretense of sophistication and am no longer embarrassed by my own actions.) When you see me, just know that I'm having a great time – listening to my favorite music and having a great day.

11

Be Appreciative.

"Two, four, six, eight. Who do we appreciate?"
High school cheer

"When you feel gratitude, you become great, and eventually attract great things."
Plato

"Gratitude is not only the greatest of virtues, but the parent of all the others."
Cicero

"...give thanks in all circumstances...."
1 Thessalonians 5:17

Who and what do you appreciate? If you're like me, you have many people and many circumstances in your life which are worthy of appreciation. Most of us have been showered with more blessings than we deserve, but we don't often take the time to let people know how much we appreciate them and how important they are in our lives. We take our friends, family, and lifestyle for granted.

One of the greatest needs that we human beings have is the need to be appreciated. Employees list "appreciation" as one of the primary things they want from their job, simply to be recognized for the contribution they make. And all of us want to feel that we are valued by others.

In turn, we must be appreciative, thankful, grateful for what we have. I've learned a lot about appreciation from a sacker at my grocery store whose name is Willie. From a career standpoint,Willie has probably reached the top level of his ability, but Willie is really good at what he does, and he appreciates the position he has.

One hot, humid August day Willie was helping me take my groceries out to the car, and I said, "Willie, aren't you just sick of this weather? It's so hot and so miserable; I'll bet you'd like to be working inside today."

Willie paused for a moment and then replied, "Every day I thank the good Lord for this job in this town at this time." While I was griping and complaining, Willie was appreciative of what he had.

Who and what do you appreciate? How long has it been since you've expressed that appreciation to the people who are important in your life or who help you on a regular basis?

Showing appreciation costs nothing but a little time and a little thoughtfulness. But expressing your appreciation not only will add joy to the lives of those who receive it but also will make you feel better in the process

12
Smile.

"I love to see you smile."
Randy Newman

*"A man without a smiling face
should never open a shop."*
Chinese proverb

*"A smile is the light in the window of your face
that tells people that your heart is at home."*
Unknown

*"Find someone who needs a smile,
and give him one of yours."*
Julie Alexander

*"Smile at each other; smile at your wife,
smile at your husband; smile at your children,
smile at each other – it doesn't matter who it is
– and that will help you to grow up in greater
love for each other."*
Mother Teresa

*"What's the use of worrying?
It never was worthwhile,
So pack up your troubles in your old kit bag,
And smile, smile, smile."*
George Asaf

"When you call me that, smile!"
Owen Wister

A smile is the most universal of expressions. Its meaning is the same in every language, so it's the international symbol of openness and acceptance. A smile says, "I acknowledge you. I accept you."

Some of us are more generous with our smiles than others. We have an unlimited supply, but some folks seem to want to horde their smiles and keep them to themselves. And most of us take our smiles for granted.

In June, 1996, *Good Morning America* did a story about a little girl named Chelsea Thomas who was born without a smile. Chelsea had a rare condition called mobius syndrome. The muscles in her face denied her the ability to smile. Chelsea desperately wanted to do what is so natural for most of us, and she made it her goal to be able to smile by her eighth birthday. After two surgeries and months of therapy, Chelsea Thomas achieved her goal. Her best birthday gift to her family, her friends, and herself was a smile.

Smiling not only brightens the day of those around you, but research shows that it even makes you feel better. When students involved in a research project were asked to contract the muscles in their faces and to frown, they started feeling angry and out of sorts. Compared to the frowners, those students who were asked to smile felt happier.

They had a more positive disposition and found jokes and cartoons funnier.

Try smiling...even when you don't feel like it. In fact, smile *especially* when you don't feel like it. You'll be surprised at the results.

Smile because...it feels good.

Smile because...it makes others feel good.

Smile because...it looks good.

Smile. It makes you look younger.

It gives you energy.

It gives you power.

It helps you gain control.

It's a stress-reliever.

Smile when you're down. It will lift your spirits.

Smile when you're angry. It will diffuse your anger and totally confuse the one who upset you.

Smile when you're frightened. It will give you courage.

Smile at yourself and say, "You're lookin' good!"

Smile for no reason other than you can.

Smile. People will wonder what you're up to.

Smile. It will put a sparkle in your eyes and joy in your heart.

Smile. It costs nothing but has tremendous value.

Smile. You have plenty to share.

Smile. It only takes a moment but the memory can last a lifetime.

Smile!

13

Get Better at Something.

"We are what we repeatedly do."
Aristotle

*"I do the very best I know how –
the very best I can; and I mean
to keep doing so until the end."*
Abraham Lincoln

*"Good, better, best,
Never let them rest;
'Til your good is better,
And your better's best."*
Julie's 8th grade English teacher

All of us need to be about the business of accomplishing something, of trying to improve in some area of our lives, and trying to be better today than we were yesterday and better tomorrow than we are today. Working toward a goal and accomplishing that goal gives us a sense of pride. We feel better about ourselves and our level of accomplishment.

Someone who truly exhibits the quality of constant improvement is my friend, Sid Mountain. Sid is in his seventies. He and his wife, Marge, live in Pagosa Springs, Colorado, and Sid could be described as a rather "colorful" character. My husband likes to say that Sid is the kind of guy who never lets the truth interfere with a good story. (Maybe you know some folks like that!) And yet, just about the time that you're convinced that Sid is pulling your leg, he comes up with some piece of evidence to prove that what he's saying is absolutely true.

Sid has had a number of interesting and unique occupations. He was a fighter pilot during World War II. He studied art in Paris; he was a minor league baseball player. He's been a college professor and a wilderness guide. But now Sid spends his time as a wildlife artist, and Sid Mountain is very good at what he does.

One of the reasons for his exceptional skill as an artist is that Sid continues on a daily basis a habit that he began when he was in his teens. Every day, without fail, Sid spends time working in his sketchbooks. The sketchbooks are amazing. There are dozens of them, a collection of years spent studying and fine-tuning his craft. On one page there are birds' wings, each feather sketched to perfection. On another, Sid has drawn the bark of trees, a study in lights and shadows. There are literally hundreds of pages on which this artist has practiced and perfected his craft.

One evening my husband and I were visiting with Sid in his studio. He was completing a very large painting, a magnificent mountain scene with an elk as its centerpiece. Being a city-dweller, a person always on a schedule and in a hurry and much too consumed with time, I said, "Sid, how long did it take you to paint that picture?" For a moment, Sid was silent. Then he looked me squarely in the eyes and said, "It has taken me 60 years."

What he meant, of course, was that it had taken him 60 years of building his skills to the point that he could create a painting like that, 60 years of working his craft, 60 years of being better today than he was yesterday and better tomorrow than he was today.

What about you? What have you done better today than the way you did it yesterday? Why just "get by" when you could be getting better?

14

Try Something New.

"When choosing between two evils, I always like to try the one I've never tried before."
Mae West

"Unless you try something beyond what you have already mastered, you will never grow."
Ralph Waldo Emerson

"You may be disappointed if you fail, but you are doomed if you do not try."
Beverly Sills

"I can accept failure, but I can't accept not trying."
Michael Jordan

Are you in a rut? Do you find yourself doing the same old things in the same old way? My former pastor, Roger McDonald, used to talk about the "everyday-ness of every day." What a perfect description of a life of sameness.

Have a great day today by trying something different. There is some truth to the old maxim which says, "Variety is the spice of life." If your life is a little bland these days, try something new. Drive to work a different way. Try a new flavor of ice cream. Go shopping, and try on some styles that you normally don't wear. Explore a part of your city that is unfamiliar. Read a section of the newspaper that you usually skip. Watch something different on television. Learn to dance. Sit with someone new at lunch. Take a trip. Buy a newspaper from another city. Park your car on the opposite side of your office building, and go in a different door. Try a new recipe. Take singing lessons. Play a different golf course. Go to a different grocery store. Try a new restaurant. Invite some new friends to your home. Rearrange your furniture. Read some magazines you don't usually read. Listen to a different radio station. Talk to strangers. Take a class. Learn a foreign language.

The world offers us many options, so try something new today.

15
Eat Something Chocolate.

(This needs no further explanation.)

16

Bite Your Tongue.

"Never say more than is necessary."
Richard Brinsley Sheridan

"Nothing is sometimes the right thing to say."
Malcolm Forbes

"When angry, count ten before you speak;
if very angry, count one hundred."
Thomas Jefferson

"When angry, count four;
when very angry, swear."
Mark Twain

The friendship between Texas oil men Clint Murchison, Sr. and Sid Richardson is legendary. In addition to their wealth, they were also known for their aphorisms which they applied to both their fishing and their business philosophy. Clint would say, "You ain't learnin' nothin' if you're talkin'," and Sid would reply, "Every fish I ever caught had its mouth open." They believed that listening and keeping one's mouth shut were two important ingredients for success.

Want to have a great day? When you're tempted to gossip, bite your tongue. When you're tempted to criticize, bite your tongue. When you want to say something mean or hurtful, bite your tongue. When your words could crush someone's spirit or damage his or her reputation, bite your tongue. When you're angry, bite your tongue. When what you want to say serves no positive purpose, bite your tongue.

Better to chew your tongue to ribbons than to say words that you will later regret.

Read.

*"I have always imagined that paradise
will be a kind of library."*
Jorge Luis Borges

*"When I get a little money, I buy books.
If any is left, I buy food and clothing."*
Erasmus

*"Outside of a dog, a man's best friend is a book;
inside of a dog, it's very dark."*
Groucho Marx

Some of my favorite places are book stores and libraries. I could, and sometimes do, spend hours just browsing the shelves – looking, skimming, enjoying the volumes of volumes. Book stores are excellent places to purchase books, and they have become gathering places for those of us who enjoy not only reading but also the pleasure of the selection process *and* a good cappuccino.

Mark Twain said, "A man who doesn't read good books has no advantage over the man who can't," and with the wealth of books that are available on every possible subject, there's no excuse for not reading.

Audio books, which are available for rental at video stores, are a God-send not only for those who are visually challenged but also for those of us who spend more time in the car than sitting in an easy chair. Books on tape make it possible to drive, garden, exercise, and still benefit from the written word in spoken form.

With the abundance of reading materials that are available, it's astonishing that so few people read. Research tells us that after high school, 58% of our society will never read a nonfiction book and that the average American reads only one book of any kind each year. Did you know that only 10% of the people who buy books will read past the first chapter? (Since you're reading this, you've made it past chapter 1. Congratulations! You're far above average!)

Harry Truman was the last American president who was not a college graduate, yet he was probably the most well-read president of modern times. By the time he was fourteen, he had read every book in the Independence, Missouri, library and had read the Bible through three times. As president he would stun his advisors, many of whom were graduates of elite universities, with his knowledge and expertise on a variety of subjects.

I know. You're saying to yourself, "But I don't have time to read." How much time do you spend watching TV or talking on the phone? The busiest of people – including the President of the United States, corporate executives, and successful entrepreneurs – are able to find 10-15 minute intervals in their fast-paced schedules to read and often read 2-3 books at the same time.

If you want to make a difference in your own life, read. If you want to make a difference in someone else's life, teach them to read. The problem of illiteracy is staggering in this country. In my state, one out of every four students can't pass the reading portion of the state standardized test required for graduation. Volunteering in a literacy program can change the lives of nonreaders and is a purposeful, productive use of your time.

Read to stay current. Read to revisit the past. Read to learn. Read for pleasure. To make it a great day, read.

Great Days

18

Mind Your Manners.

"A well-mannered person is not one who knows which fork to use first, but one who doesn't notice when others use the wrong one."
Anton Chekhov

Whenever people talk about my mother, they always describe her as being a "lady," a term not used too often in today's society. She is, indeed, a lovely, gentle, caring, and totally unselfish person whose thoughts are always focused on the needs of others.

Mother's thoughtful notes written to congratulate, encourage, or console are legendary. She was a kindergarten teacher for sixteen years, and whenever she reads or hears about the accomplishments of her former students, she sends a congratulatory note. Her students are delighted to receive a letter from their first teacher who has never forgotten them and who cares enough to stay in touch.

My mother has a way of helping to heal the sorrows of friends and family with her gentle gestures of thoughtfulness. She is the personification of kindness, is non-judgmental, accepting, forgiving, and loves unconditionally. With all these "soft" qualities, she is also spunky, has a great sense of humor, and is fiercely independent. Her greatest concern is that she will be a burden to someone else.

My mother's selflessness is truly refreshing in a time when rudeness has become commonplace. In a society with little regard for rules, politeness is the exception. Most people try to get their way by bullying, perhaps thinking that ranting, raving, and causing a scene is the only way to get what they want. Actually, I've found that just the opposite is true. Politeness is now so rare that those who operate from that stance place themselves in a powerful position.

In Harvey Mackay's book *Dig Your Well Before You're Thirsty,* Mackay says that being polite makes you, what he calls, a "differentiator," a person set apart from the pack. He also points out that having manners is simply being considerate of the feelings of others. It's interesting, isn't it, that corporations spend millions of dollars each year training their employees in "customer service," when in reality, customer service is nothing more than being polite and showing consideration for the needs and feelings of others.

I've discovered that those people who resolve disputes by being polite and well-mannered have the upper hand. The right combination of firmness, confidence, and calm politeness – delivered with a smile – is hard to beat. Our manners are really a reflection of our spirit, and good manners reflect a gentleness and a desire for fairness and harmony that quite often will get us what we want. As the old adage reminds us, we can, indeed, catch more flies with honey than with vinegar.

In my mother's case, her manners are motivated by her genuine thoughtfulness. Some of the rest of us, who aren't blessed with such a gentle spirit, have to work at it a little harder. But the reward is worth the effort.

19

Risk.

"To win you have to risk loss."
Jean-Claude Killy

"Progress means taking risks, for you can't steal home and keep your foot on third base."
Herbert V. Prochnow

"Take calculated risks. That is quite different from being rash."
Gen. George Patton

"The chief danger in life is that you may take too many precautions."
Alfred Adler

"Risk! Risk anything! Care no more for the opinions of others. Do the hardest thing on earth for you. Act for yourself."
Katherine Mansfield

"Do the thing you fear, and the death of fear is certain."
Ralph Waldo Emerson

Most regrets that people have in life are regrets not of what they did but what they didn't do. Because we aren't willing to risk, there are great ideas that are never acted upon, fascinating people who are never met, adventures that are never taken, experiences that are never experienced. We miss out on so many of life's opportunities because we are afraid. We're afraid to try, afraid to ask, afraid to take the risk that is a necessary component of any bold action.

I have to admit that for most of my life, I've been a chicken, a wimp, a coward. In describing myself, I would have to use all those unsavory words that characterize someone who's fearful, overly cautious, and unwilling to take a chance. But I've discovered that some of the most rewarding circumstances in life are those which have come when I've stepped out on a limb and taken a risk.

In the summer of 1992, my husband and I and two other couples were invited to be among a group of adult guests at Frontier Ranch, a camp near Buena Vista, Colorado. This incredible facility is sponsored by Young Life, a nondenominational Christian organization which ministers to teens. As adult guests, we were encouraged to participate in all the activities that the campers were doing – horseback riding, hiking, and some other adventures which proved to be considerably more challenging.

One of the scariest experiences for me was rappelling. Rappelling involves being strapped into a harness and descending down the side of a mountain by controlling a series of ropes.

Quite frankly, I was scared to death. I'd known that this activity would be scheduled for sometime during our week's stay but didn't know what day of the week it would be. Monday came and went – no rappelling. Tuesday – still no rappelling. Tuesday night I couldn't sleep. I was convinced that Wednesday would be the day. But again on Wednesday and Thursday, no rappelling…and no sleep. (Maybe they'd forgotten. I could always hope.) And then came Friday. They hadn't forgotten. Rappelling day had arrived.

There were twelve adults in our group, and I discovered that I wasn't the only one who had cowardly tendencies. Two of the other women and one man announced that they weren't going to participate.They were going to stay on the ground and take pictures. Great idea, I thought. I'm *really good* at taking pictures! I'll stay with them!

If you think that teenagers are the only ones who are subjected to peer pressure, you're wrong. The others in the group – my husband, my friends, and all the other brave (or foolish) adults – began to pressure, ridicule, and harass me, and I finally agreed to go. I guess I feared the humiliation more than the rappelling.

The nine of us began the long climb up the mountain. About a third of the way up, we found a large wooden chest beside the trail, and inside the chest were helmets. For some reason I've never been attracted to any activity which requires a helmet. For me, a helmet says, "This is dangerous and hazardous to your health." Why was there no warning label from the surgeon general? Foolishly, we donned the helmets and continued up the trail.

After a long and fairly difficult climb, we reached the top. The rappelling instructors were waiting for us – cheerful, confident. What was wrong with these people? Down on the ground were the three photographers smiling and waving, and at this moment I understood why they looked so happy. Would that I were with them!

The instructors gave us a basic lesson in rappelling – how the ropes worked, what to do, what not to do. Not enough instruction I felt sure, because all too soon it was time for the dreaded "leap of faith." I'd learned from other experiences that the longer one waits, the more anxious one becomes, so I decided to be among the first to volunteer. Besides, I wanted to be done with it.

As I was getting into the harness, I thought about my family and friends. I wondered what dress my husband would choose to bury me in and who would come to my funeral. I tried to be very logical. My head told me that this had to be safe or the camp's lawyers wouldn't allow such an activity, but that logical thinking didn't calm my fears.

All too soon, it was time. It was my turn. There would be no more delays and certainly no turning back at this point. And so, with supporters on the mountain and photographers on the ground, I smiled...took a step backwards off the edge of the cliff, and I was on my way.

What an experience! It was wonderful! Suddenly I was having the time of my life, bouncing off the side of the mountain and swinging out the full extent of the rope. And as I came down, I saw the photographers, the ones who hadn't dared, the ones who didn't risk...and I felt sorry for them. They'd missed it. They'd missed an experience of a lifetime because they were afraid, and they had let their fears rob them of an incredible opportunity.

That event was a turning point for me. It demonstrated the benefits we receive when we take a risk. As a reminder, in my office I keep a picture of myself taken the day of that adventure, and I look at it when I'm in need of encouragement to get out of my comfort zone and to try something that's difficult or scary.

In September, 1993, I shared this story in a seminar that I presented to a group of executive secretaries at a large insurance company in Missouri, and in 1994, I received an inspiring letter from Robyn Roberts who had attended that seminar. Here's what Robyn told me:

"When you spoke at our company, you told us to take a risk, so I wanted to tell you what you inspired me to do.

"As you know, in January, 1994, Los Angeles experienced a major earthquake. My company asked for volunteers to go to L.A. as part of the catastrophe team to help settle the thousands of insurance claims from the victims of that disaster. I have been married for fifteen of my thirty-two years. I moved directly from my parents' care to that of my husband. I had never been on my own. I had never been any further west than Kansas City, had never been on an airplane, and had never been in a city the size of Los Angeles, but I volunteered to go.

"For six long weeks I drove the Pacific coast highway from San Juan Capistrano north to Santa Barbara. I experienced aftershocks that rocked the air conditioner unit off my hotel wall. On my own, I visited Pepperdine University and cruised to Catalina. I watched surfers, whales, and dolphins and saw and experienced things that were totally new to me. When my husband and my children visited me on my weekend off, they were amazed at my ability to maneuver the airport

traffic and to chauffeur them to Disneyland and Universal Studios.

"Needless to say, this experience was a big risk for me, but I feel terrific about myself! I feel like a new, more confident, poised person! I have five classes left to complete my Bachelor of Arts in Management, and I'm looking into many career possibilities with my company.

"Thanks for your advice about risk-taking. I am confident I will be a success at whatever the future offers."

What a great letter! Robyn discovered, as you will, too, that when you step out and take a risk in one area of your life, it will give you confidence to risk in others.

What do you want or need to do that requires a risk? I'd recommend that every day you do something that makes you sweat – something that's a little difficult, a little challenging, something that involves mustering your courage and reaching out beyond your comfort zone. You may surprise yourself at what you can do. Remember, turtles can't get anywhere without sticking out their necks; maybe the same is true for us.

Am I always courageous? Have I changed from being a coward to a dare-devil? Do I take the leap every time with no hesitation or fear? Certainly not. There are many times when I'm afraid to risk. I'm unwilling to chance loss or embarrassment or failure. But nine times out of ten, when I muster my courage and am willing to risk, I'm rewarded with feelings of self-confidence to take on other challenges. The same can happen for you.

20

Do Something Nice for Someone.

"No one is useless in this world who lightens the burden of it to anyone else."
Charles Dickens

"Unless life is lived for others, it is not worthwhile."
Mother Teresa

"You give but little when you give possessions; it is when you give of yourself that you truly give."
Kahlil Gibran

"I tell you the truth, whatever you did for one of the least of these brothers of mine, you did for me."
Matthew 25:40

"You never reach your full potential if you think you exist for yourself."
Unknown

One of the best ways to guarantee a great day is to focus your attention on someone else. Several years ago the spirit of "Random Acts of Kindness" captured the imagination of the country. What a simple, yet powerful, concept – the idea of doing something nice for someone with no expectations of anything in return.

I had the radio on one morning as I was getting dressed. I was listening for a weather forecast, the temperature, and the traffic report. It was a cold, windy morning, and a heavy, unexpected rain had snarled traffic all over the city.

As I listened, a caller telephoned the radio station on his cellular phone to report something he had just witnessed. Several people were standing at a bus stop in the torrential downpour. Since the storm had not been predicted, they had no protection from the rain and were getting soaked. One woman was holding her purse above her head, as if it would protect her from the elements and keep her dry.

The caller reported that he had watched as a car pulled up beside the people on the curb. The driver had jumped out of his car, handed them an umbrella, and then gotten back into the car, quickly moved into the flow of traffic, and was gone. The caller was touched by what he had seen and wanted to share the story of that simple, yet benevolent, gesture with those of us who were listening.

What a beautiful example of doing something for someone else. I recently read,

"Share an umbrella with someone, and your heart will be filled with sunshine." The giver of the umbrella that morning surely had a heart filled not only with sunshine but also with love and compassion for his fellow man.

What can you do for someone today? What kind of "umbrella" can you provide? A smile, a listening ear, a little time, a word of encouragement or appreciation? There are many different kinds of umbrellas that can shelter people from the storms of life.

Erma Bombeck was a one-of-a-kind talent, a woman whose wit, warmth, and wisdom were a national treasure. Erma once wrote, "My deeds will be measured not by my youthful appearance, but by the concern lines on my forehead, the laugh lines around my mouth, and the chins from seeing what can be done for those smaller than me or those who have fallen." What a lovely description of compassion.

You have the power to create great days for yourself and everyone with whom you come in contact by focusing your attention on them and sharing a little of your time, your compassion, and your heart. Today and every day, be ready to share umbrellas with those who need them.

21

Do Something
Nice for Yourself.

"I use L'Oreal; I'm worth it."
L'Oreal commercial

*"All I ask is that you treat me no differently
than you would the Queen."*
Seen on a T-shirt

*"I did not have three thousand pairs of shoes.
I had one thousand and sixty."*
Imelda Marcos

All of us need to indulge ourselves a little, so do something nice for yourself today. Take a nap. Get a pedicure. Go to a movie. Don't answer the phone. Take a walk in the park. Go fishing. Have a picnic. Buy yourself some flowers. Go shopping. Enjoy the company of your best friend. Put your feet in a mountain stream. Eat chocolate. Take a bubble bath. Get a massage. Create something. Buy a new pair of shoes. Take time to do whatever it is that you *love* to do...and have a great day!

22

Learn the Real Meaning of Success.

"To laugh often and much; to win the respect of intelligent people and the affection of children; to earn the appreciation of honest critics and endure the betrayal of false friends; to appreciate beauty; to find the best in others; to leave the world a bit better, whether by a healthy child, a garden patch or a redeemed social condition; to know even one life has breathed easier because you lived. This is to have succeeded."

Ralph Waldo Emerson

23

Get Excited About Something.

"Man is only truly great when he acts from passion."
Benjamin Disraeli

"Men who never get carried away should be."
Malcolm Forbes

"Nothing great was ever achieved without enthusiasm."
Ralph Waldo Emerson

"If you aren't fired up with enthusiasm, you will be fired with enthusiasm."
Vince Lombardi

I love to be around people who are excited about something, don't you? They seem to generate energy for themselves and everyone with whom they come in contact. Their enthusiasm, their energy, their excitement, their passion is contagious.

How depressing and boring it is to be subjected to those folks who never get excited about anything. You know who they are. They are the ones who never like a restaurant, are unimpressed by any movie or play, find fault with all destinations and traveling companions, and are generally unmoved by everything.

Give me the person who finds joy and delight in the little things as well as the big ones. Let me be in the company of those who are passionate about something – a cause, a hobby, a sport, their work, music, their loved ones. The person with passion and excitement is the one who has power and makes things happen; that kind of person is the spark that lights a fire in the hearts of others. As the French philosopher La Rochefoucauld wrote, "The passions are the only advocates which always persuade. The simplest man with passion will be more persuasive than the most eloquent without."

What are you excited about today? What is your passion? Great days belong to those who live enthusiastically.

24

Give Out What You Want to Get Back.

"...for whatever a man sows,
that will he also reap."
Galatians 6:7

"Do to others what you
would have them do to you."
Matthew 7:12

"We have committed the Golden Rule to memory;
We must now commit it to life."
Edwin Markham

"What goes around comes around."
Unknown

While stopped at a traffic light one day, I couldn't help but notice the little girl who was peering out the back window of the car in front of me. She looked disgruntled, out of sorts, and mad at the world. It was obvious that she was not having a great day. She could see that I was watching her, and she glared back at me.

I decided to have a little fun with her and responded to her scowl in an unexpected way. I smiled...not much of a smile, just a little one that said, "I see you." She was not amused, and she retaliated by sticking out her tongue and making a face at me. I just smiled back at her, a much bigger, warmer smile this time. It was obvious that she didn't know what to make of this crazy woman who responded to her in such an unexpected way. She was stumped, unsure of what to do next.

I just continued to smile, and then I waved at her. Now the ball was in her court. It was her turn to make a move, and I couldn't wait to see what she would do next. Suddenly, she disappeared out of view, but when she reappeared, she was holding up her doll for me to see...and she was smiling. We do, indeed, get back what we send out.

According to the history books, Dolley Madison, wife of President James Madison, was a delightful woman who was known not only for her hospitality but also for her warmth and genuine concern for others. She treated everyone with dignity and respect. When told that "everybody loves Mrs. Madison," Dolley quickly replied, "Mrs. Madison loves everybody." That's usually the way it works, isn't it?

My dad was the most positive person I've ever known. Whenever I think of him, I see him smiling. He was the kind of person that people were drawn to because he radiated a cheerfulness, a love of life, and a sincere interest in others. Like Dolley Madison, my dad liked everyone, and they liked him in return. His friends and acquaintances were a study in diversity of race, religion, age, education, and income, and one of the reasons that they liked him was that he never seemed to notice the differences; to him they were just folks, and he treated them all with kindness, respect, and loving compassion.

I read something one time that said if you're dog-tired when you come home at night, maybe it's because you've been growling all day. The wisdom of the Golden Rule still holds true today. If you want to have great days, what you give is what you'll get.

25

Pray.

"...pray continually..."
1 Thessalonians 5:17

"Is any one of you in trouble?
He should pray."
James 5:13

"Pray for each other so that you may be healed.
The prayer of a righteous man
is powerful and effective."
James 5:16b

"Be not forgetful of prayer. Every time you pray,
if your prayer is sincere, there will be
new feeling and new meaning in it, which will
give you fresh courage, and you will under-
stand that prayer is an education."
Fyodor Dostoyevsky

To have great days, spend a part of every day in prayer. Through prayer we find peace, comfort, encouragement, strength, and hope to face the challenges that each day brings. Prayer also provides us with an opportunity to be thankful and to express gratitude for our many blessings. Want to have great days? Spend some time talking with and listening to your Creator.

26

Listen.

*"A man can learn a heap of things
if he keeps his ears clean."*
Unknown

*"Nature has given us two ears
but only one mouth."*
Benjamin Disraeli

*"A wise old owl sat on an oak,
The more he saw the less he spoke;
The less he spoke the more he heard;
Why aren't we like that wise old bird?"*
Edward Hersey Richards

W hen we think of communicating with people, we usually think about the talking, but perhaps the most important part of communication is the listening. Most of us aren't too good at that. We're so busy thinking about what we're going to say that we can hardly wait for the other person to finish.

Have you ever noticed that some people have "selective hearing?" They hear only what they choose to hear and ignore the rest. My father-in-law had serious hearing loss due to an accident in childhood. His condition worsened as he aged, but we often thought that he could hear more than he acknowledged. He seemed to be especially skilled at tuning out his wife.

When my mother-in-law and father-in-law celebrated their fiftieth wedding anniversary, the family honored them with a reception. One of the guests was talking with my father-in-law, and he asked, "Well, Vic, what's the secret of being married for fifty years?" My father-in-law cupped his hand around his good ear, leaned forward, and said, "What'd you say?" to which the guest responded, "That's the secret!"

Perhaps the greatest compliment that we can pay to another person is to really listen to what he or she is saying, to focus our attention, and to tune in not only to the words but also to the unspoken message, which often is where the true meaning lies.

Margaret Bourke-White was known not only as a famous photographer for *Life* magazine but also for her ability to focus her attention on people as skillfully as she focused her camera. An admirer said that his interest in her was the result of her interest in him. She knew how to listen and how to concentrate sincere attention on others.

In her book *Listening: The Forgotten Skill*, Madelyn Burley-Allen tells a story of two men who were walking along the crowded sidewalk of a busy, downtown street. Suddenly, one of the men exclaimed, "Listen to the lovely sound of that cricket!" The other had no idea what he was talking about. He couldn't hear the sound of a cricket amidst the roar of people and traffic. The story goes on, "The first man, who was a zoologist, had trained himself to listen to the voices of nature, but he did not explain. He simply took a coin out of his pocket and dropped it on the sidewalk, whereupon a dozen people began to glance about them, looking for the dropped coin. 'We hear,' he said, 'what we listen for.'"

What are you listening for? Are you listening for the real message that is being sent to you, or are you so focused on yourself that your voice is all you hear?

To have a great day, remember that the key element in communication is listening. Really listen to people. Listen to your children, your grandchildren, your spouse, your family, your co-workers, your customers, your friends by looking into their eyes and focusing your attention on them. Perhaps they will learn from your example and listen to you when you want to be heard. Listening to another person with your ears, your eyes, your mind, and your heart is the best way to say to the people in your life, "You are important," and of course, they are.

27

Work.

"Sweat never drowned no one."
Unknown

*"To be successful, the first thing to do
is fall in love with your work."*
Sister Mary Lauretta

*"I'm against retiring. The thing that keeps a
man alive is having something to do. Sitting in a
rocker never appealed to me. Golf or fishing isn't
as much fun as working."*
Colonel Harlan Sanders

*"I like work; it fascinates me.
I can sit and look at it for hours."*
Jerome K. Jerome

Work has gotten a bad reputation. In fact, some people believe that this four-letter word is the curse of humanity. Recently a major news magazine's cover story was entitled "Work is Hell." I disagree. Work is a wonderful thing. It is work that not only provides us with income but also adds to our personal identity. It gives us a reason to get up in the morning, a purpose, an opportunity to make a contribution to the world. Work is a blessing. If you don't believe it, just ask someone who's unemployed or disabled and can't work.

Admittedly some jobs are less rewarding than others. If you talk to the average person who fights the rush hour traffic each day to get to a job that's boring and unfulfilling, that lacks challenge and excitement, and that provides a minimum wage, he may say he'd rather spend his time doing nothing. But after awhile, too much leisure becomes even more boring and unfulfilling than unsatisfying work.

What would you do if you inherited a huge fortune or won the lottery? Would you continue to work? In his book *The Pursuit of Happiness*, Dr. David G. Myers reveals that a University of Michigan study found that 3 out of 4 people said "yes"; they would continue to work even if they were suddenly blessed with great wealth, and nearly all who enjoy the nonmaterial rewards of work – a sense of identity, community, and purpose – gave a positive response. They said they would keep right on working at their current job even if Ed McMahon came to their door with a million dollar prize!

Work has many definitions. It's the physical or mental effort or activity directed toward the production or accomplishment of something. It's the means by which one earns one's livelihood. What is your work? Perhaps your work is in a corporation or in a classroom. Perhaps you work as a programmer, a researcher, a salesperson, a medical technician. Perhaps you're an engineer or a librarian, a manager or a flight attendant, a waiter or a physician. Perhaps you work as a volunteer in a hospital or a homeless shelter or work shaping lives as a parent. Whatever your work is, appreciate it and be thankful for it.

My mother believes that work is therapeutic, and she's right. She says that if you're lonely, sad, or depressed, you should go to work, i.e., get busy doing *something*. Even cleaning out a closet, weeding the garden, or rearranging the garage can take your mind off your problems and provide you with a productive, worthwhile activity.

Be grateful for work, It's not only a gift but also an opportunity to serve humanity. In his book *Being God's Partner*, Jeffrey K. Salkin says that God wants us to do our work in a certain way and that our work is part of our religious orientation to the world. Rabbi Salkin suggests that we look at our work in a new way and realize that we are "God's partners in the seemingly mundane world of nine-to-five." What a fresh way of looking at the work we do and understanding its purpose in the overall scheme of things.

Whatever your work is, whether it's done for a fee or for free, do that work, even if it seems mundane, to the best of your ability. Martin Luther King, Jr. said, "If a man is called to be a street sweeper, he should sweep streets even as Michaelangelo painted, or Beethoven composed music, or Shakespeare wrote poetry. He should sweep streets so well that all the hosts of heaven and earth will pause to say, 'Here lived a great street sweeper who did his job well.'"

Want to have great days? Then work at something. Fill your time with purposeful work purposefully done, and be grateful for the opportunity to serve.

28

Rest.

*"To do great work, one must be very idle
as well as very industrious."*
Samuel Butler

"Rest and be thankful."
Inscription on a stone seat in the Scottish Highlands

"Be still and know that I am God."
Psalm 46:10

We need to work, but we also need to rest. Great days are the result of fulfilling, satisfying work and renewing rest. Rest is a mental and physical recess from the stress of work and obligations. Rest is not only sleep but also time spent in solitude, in play, in the company of nurturing friends, and each of these is critical to a balanced life.

We live in a frenzied, fast-paced world. We are overwhelmed, plagued with too much to do and not enough time to do it. There never seems to be time to escape to a quiet oasis of peace and solitude.

Take some time today to rest, to think, to regroup, to rest your body and your spirit.

29
Play.

"All work and no play makes Jack a dull boy."
Unknown

*"Although we need to work for physical
survival, we need to play to make
survival worthwhile."*
Eda LaShan

*"Work consists of whatever a body is obliged to
do...Play consists of whatever a body
is not obliged to do."*
Mark Twain

L ike work and rest, play is a necessity
of life, and it's great therapy. Anything
that you enjoy doing and do just for
fun can be considered play.

Play is active leisure, and active leisure
has been shown to be much more beneficial
and renewing than passive leisure, i.e., plop-
ping down in front of the television. Watching programs which focus on acts of violence,
brutality, hatred and abuse, and "comedies"
based on put-down humor, dysfunctional
relationships, and sarcastic cynicism is more
stressful than restful. Radio personality Fred
Allen said of television in its early years, "It
is a device that allows people with nothing

to do to watch people who can't do anything." Not much has changed.

If you choose to spend your leisure time watching television, be selective in your viewing. But if you want to use your limited time for play to really renew your body and your spirit, choose activities that "involve" you, both physically and mentally. Walk, read, garden, play games with your family and friends, take a class, play golf, paint, refinish furniture, bake bread, learn a foreign language, go fishing, sing in a choir, play a musical instrument. Perhaps you're thinking that these things sound more like work than play. Actually it is in participating in activities like these that one finds the greatest satisfaction and sense of renewal.

Find some time each day to play, and when you do, play with the enthusiasm of a child. In fact, childlike play can be lots of fun for adults. How long has it been since you played hop-scotch, jumped rope, slid down a slide, played on a see-saw, flew a kite, blew bubbles, ran through a lawn sprinkler, waded in a stream, had a pillow fight?

To have great days, we need a balance of work, rest, and play, because "the magic is in the mix."

30

Get Your Priorities in Order.

"Things that matter most must never be at the mercy of things which matter least."
Goethe

"The best things in life aren't things."
Unknown

On May 11, 1996, Beck Weathers, a Dallas pathologist with a passion for high adventure, survived a tragic, terrifying day on Mt. Everest. Eight of his fellow climbers did not survive. Weathers' much-publicized story of being separated from his party, wandering alone on the mountain, enduring temperatures of perhaps 50 below zero and 70-knot winds, and being left for dead is the stuff of best-selling novels and Hollywood mega-movies. But for this man, it was not fiction but harsh reality.

Although Beck Weathers survived this ordeal, he lost his right arm almost to the elbow. The fingers and most of the thumb of his left hand had to be removed, and surgeons constructed a new nose to replace the one lost to frostbite, but Weathers considers himself fortunate – fortunate, certainly, to be alive, but fortunate, too, to have been given the chance to see life in a new light and to get a new vision of what really matters.

As a man obsessed with reaching the summit of both his career and his mountain-climbing goals, Weathers admits that he had lost sight of what really mattered in life, particularly his family. His time was spent either working or working out. Possessed by both his profession and his passion for adventure, there was no time for the ones who cared for him and who needed him most. His relationship with his wife was breaking down; he hardly knew his children. He was losing his family. They were the victims of his ambitious and selfish obsessions.

Since that tragic day on the mountain and his amazing survival, Beck Weathers now has his priorities in order. He's found a peace that had once eluded him, and he feels that he traded his hands for his family and his future. The trade, he says, was worth the price.

In a story in the *Dallas Morning News* written one year after his rescue, Beck Weathers said, "In one of those old movies – maybe it was *The Wizard of Oz* – they talk about these things that you dream and you pursue, and you go out and see if you can find this thing that in some way, validates you and makes you whole. And then when all is said and done, you come back, and you discover that it was in your own backyard the whole time."

The most important things in life are usually found close to home – our families, our friends, our faith. Unfortunately some of us find out too late that it is the relationships in life – not fame, fortune, awards, or achievement – which really matter.

Who and what is most important in your life? Are you focusing your time and attention on them, or are you attempting to climb mountains that bring little reward upon reaching the top? Create great days for yourself and those you love by spending time together, by creating strong relationships and treasured memories, by valuing those things that have the most value.

Great Days

31

Be a Chin-lifter.

*"Our chief want in life is someone who will
inspire us to be what we already
know we could be."*
Ralph Waldo Emerson

*"Keep away from people who try to belittle
your ambitions. Small people always do that,
but the really great make you feel that you,
too, can be great."*
Mark Twain

*"Therefore, encourage one another and build
each other up, just as in fact you are doing."*
1 Thessalonians 5:11

"Everybody is somebody's cheerleader."
Julie Alexander

When I was in junior high and high school, I wanted to be a cheerleader. I wanted to wear one of those cute little cheerleader outfits, run up and down the sidelines, shake my pompons, and encourage the team to victory. I never got to do that. I've finally accepted that youthful disappointment, but not long ago I realized that, in reality, everybody is somebody's cheerleader. Each one of us has the opportunity every day to be a cheerleader to someone – to our spouses, our children, our colleagues, our friends – and part of our mission in life should be to find ways to be cheerleaders, to give encouragement to those who are in need of an emotional boost.

One night when our youngest son, Ben, was about 12 years old, I was tucking him into bed, and we were having what might be called a "pre-go-to-bed" pep rally. I was telling him how much we loved him, how proud we were of him, and how we felt that he was making the right decisions and doing the right things. Ben lay quietly in his bed listening to all this. Then he said, "Mom, you know how you're always telling me about how much you love me and care about me and all that other stuff? Sometimes when I'm having a bad day at school, I think about that, and it helps." Maybe I'm a cheerleader after all.

Several years ago my mother was in the hospital with a very serious illness. Fortunately, she had doctors and nurses who not only cared for her but also cheered her up and helped her get through a very difficult time. But the interesting thing was that my mother, too, was a cheerleader for so many people in that hospital.

There was an aide who was trying to decide what to do with her life, and my mother encouraged her to stay in school and to get her education. There was a physical therapist who was having some marital problems, and my mother encouraged her to be strong and courageous. It's never too late for all of us to be cheerleaders, even if we missed out on the pompons.

In the early years of my speaking career, I attended a convention of the National Speakers Association. The members of this organization are professionals in the truest sense of the word. They earn their livings as speakers and are among the best known and most successful presenters in the country. Since the convention was held in my home-town, I could attend the sessions during the day and come home at night.

I was on an emotional roller coaster the entire week of the convention. Being around those successful speakers, people whom I had admired from afar, was overwhelming. The educational sessions were packed with information on how to build one's career and success stories of those who were at the top of the profession. The first few days, I came home from the convention filled with excite-ment and sure that I, too, could be successful in this challenging business. But later in the week, I was feeling overwhelmed, depressed, and convinced that I had no chance of ful-filling my dream.

On one of the "down" days of the conven-tion, when I was feeling particularly discouraged, our oldest son greeted me at the back door when I arrived home. He could tell that something was wrong. There was no excitement, no sparkle on this day. "What's the matter, Mom?" he asked.

"Oh, Adam, I just don't think I have what it takes to make it. Everyone else is so good. They're so polished and so smart about running their businesses. Why did I ever think I could do this? I think maybe I should just give up this whole notion of becoming a speaker!"

At that point, my son did something for me that I will never forget – he lifted my chin. And he said, "Mom, you can do it. Just keep working and keep trying, and I think you're going to make it." All of us need "chin-lifters" in our lives, those people who believe in us even when we don't believe in ourselves.

I've been fortunate to have many "chin-lifters" in my life. My husband, Ken, has always believed in me and "been there" for me. My sons have been a source of encouragement. I had parents who supported me and am blessed with special loving friends who lift my spirits.

I hope that you have lots of "chin-lifters" in your life. Certainly the best way to get some is to first be one. Be a chin-lifter today to those around you. The word "encourage" means to inspire, to impart courage or confidence; embolden; hearten. And encouragement does, indeed, come from the hearts of those who care.

Great Days

32

Ban Boredom.

*"A bore is someone who, when you
ask him how he is, tells you."*
Unknown

*"Any idiot can handle a crisis. It's the day to
day living that wears you out."*
Anton Chekhov

U ntil he retired a few years ago, Tony
Lepone worked as a traffic cop in
Providence, Rhode Island. His job
was to stand in the middle of an intersection
and direct traffic, and after a time, that became boring – same intersection, same
traffic, same rude drivers. Tony was becoming frustrated with his "everydayness of every
day," and he decided to do something different, something that would eliminate the
boredom and make his work more fun. So
Tony started dancing as he signaled. Standing in the middle of the intersection, Tony
gyrated, swirled, moved his arms, and
swayed to the music, entertaining himself
and having a great time. Tony Lepone took
responsibility for his boredom and took it
upon himself to make his work more interesting and a lot more fun.

Of course, as is usually the case, Tony's
enthusiasm was contagious. The motorists

and pedestrians who passed through his intersection loved the show! Seeing Tony dancing and having fun made them smile and added enjoyment to their day as well. People started telling their friends and co-workers, and pretty soon folks were driving through the intersection just to get a look at Tony Lepone, the dancing cop. *Good Morning America* heard about him and featured him in a special report. In Providence, Rhode Island, Tony Lepone was a celebrity, all because he refused to be bored by a boring job.

When Margaret White was 98 years old, she was living alone in her mobile home in the Oklahoma panhandle, and life wasn't too exciting. Although Margaret was in good health, she was bored. "I was about ready to give up," Margaret said. "I just didn't care about nothin'. But then," she said, "I started shot-putting." At age 98 Margaret took up the shot-put! Her son taught her how to throw the 8.8 pound shot, and Margaret had found her sport, something she was good at and something that made her days more interesting. She said she did it mainly "just to keep myself limbered up," but after awhile, she began to enjoy both the activity and the challenge.

When Margaret was 100 years old, she entered a senior track and field event. She not only won a gold medal but also set a new world record...in her age category!

Are you bored? If so, take responsibility for your boredom and do something about it. We live in a fascinating world. There's so much to do, so many things to learn, so much to experience. Like Tony and Margaret, you can make your life more interesting and fun.

Great Days

33

Accept and Embrace Change.

*"The only person who likes change
is a wet baby."*
Ray Blitzer

*"Change is inevitable...
except from a vending machine."*
Bumper sticker

"The future ain't what it used to be."
Casey Stengel

We live in a rapidly changing world. Things aren't the same today as they were yesterday, and they won't be tomorrow as they are today. We literally wake up in a brand new world every day. The amazing advances in technology provide us with the ability to do things and know things that were unheard of just a few short years ago. I have to admit that, in terms of technology, I'm not the sharpest knife in the drawer, but I'm making a real effort to at least become computer literate. I realize that if I don't learn these new skills, I'll be left in the dust. Besides, these days *everybody* is high-tech. Even the Vatican has a Web site!

At a luncheon in Waco, Texas, I had the pleasure of sitting next to a lovely lady named Clara Fentress. During our visit, Clara proudly informed me that she was 94 years old. At the end of the meal, this charming writer and conversationalist suggested that we stay in touch. As I started to write down my mailing address for her, Clara asked, "Don't you have e-mail?" It turns out that Clara communicates regularly with her family and friends over the Internet. What an inspiration to all of us to embrace the changes in technology.

But our lives change, too. If you want a verification that change is taking place, look in the mirror. That's enough to shock us into the realities of change. Our lives do change. Our children grow up. Relationships and circumstances change. What once we took for granted – in terms of lifestyle or career or friendships or health – change, and while we may view some of those changes as positive, others we may consider more negative. Such is the stuff of life.

Have you ever gone into your favorite grocery store and discovered that all the items have been moved to a different location? When you look for the dog food, you find that it's where the soup used to be, and the laundry detergent is now where the cereal was? How does that make you feel? Most of us react negatively to this situation. These changes are frustrating, irritating, and uncomfortable. They force us to get out of our routine, go in a different direction, and explore new areas. But after awhile, we get used to the new arrangement of the store. We often have a hard time remembering "how it used to be." We adapt.

Life is like that. Changes take place, changes that we don't always want or welcome. Some of those changes cause us to need to take action, to learn some new skills, to embrace the changes and make the most of them. As things change, we often have to just make the decision that we will accept these changes and grow from them. Dr. Carl Hammerschlag says, "Growth has nothing to do with adding things on but of letting go." And the letting go is often the most difficult.

It's interesting, though, that we human beings have an amazing capacity to adapt. Most people who suffer tragedy or tremendous loss or pain, eventually adapt. The scars may remain; the pain of the loss may not be forgotten, but there is an eventual "return to normalcy" which proves our power to get used to a new situation. Shortly after her husband died suddenly and unexpectedly, a young mother of three was told by another young widow, "I know that right now you think you'll never be happy again. You think there'll never be a day when you'll be able to smile and honestly say, 'This has been a good day,' but you will. Trust me; you *will* be happy again." And sure enough, the time came when she was. Just as we learn the new location of items in the grocery store, we learn new patterns of behavior with our changed circumstances. We adapt.

To have great days we must realize that change, whether positive or negative, is inevitable, and our only defense is to embrace some of the changes and accept the others.

34

Value Words of Wisdom.

"Wisdom is supreme; therefore get wisdom."
Proverbs 4:7

"He who walks with the wise grows wise..."
Proverbs 13:20

When President James A. Garfield was a young man, an elderly friend and mentor gave him some "words of wisdom" that Garfield would cherish all his life. These were his personal principles upon which he built a successful life. Following Garfield's "Rules for Living" will certainly increase your chances of having great days.

- Never be idle.

- Make few promises.

- Always speak the truth.

- Live within your income.

- Never speak evil of anyone.

- Keep good company or none.

- Live up to your engagements.

- Never play games of chance.

- Drink no intoxicating drinks.

- Good character is above anything else.

- Keep your own secrets if you have any.

- Never borrow if you can possibly help it.

- Do not marry until you are able to support a wife.

- When you speak to a person, look into his eyes.

- Save when you are young to spend when you are old.

- Never run into debt unless you see a way out again.

- Good company and good conversation are the sinews of virtue.

- Your character cannot be essentially injured except by your own acts.

- If anybody speaks evil of you, let your life be so that no one believes him.

- When you retire at night, think over what you have done during the day.

- If your hands cannot be employed usefully, attend to the culture of your mind.

- Read the above carefully and thoughtfully at least once a week.

GREAT DAYS

35

Eat Something *Else* Chocolate!

Great Days

36

Focus on Others.

*"If you are all wrapped up in yourself,
you are overdressed."*
Kate Halverson

*"Seek first to understand,
then to be understood."*
Stephen Covey

Perhaps one of the best ways to have great days is to focus our attention on other people. We tend to think that our problems, our concerns, our ideas, our needs are the most important. But when we begin to focus on others, we become less self-centered and more self-less. Our problems seem to diminish when we turn our thoughts to those around us.

If you're in the dumps and feeling a little depressed or out of sorts, if you're feeling sorry for yourself, look around. There are so many others whose condition is worse than yours. When you're feeling blue, forget yourself and concentrate on what you can do for someone else. It's a sure way to improve your day...and theirs, too.

37

Have a Sense of Humor.

*"The joy of joys is a person of light
but unmalicious humor."*
Emily Post

"If you're too busy to laugh, you're too busy."
Unknown

*"Laugh and the world laughs with you,
But you stay after school alone."*
Unknown

*"If you wish to glimpse inside a human soul
and get to know a man...just watch him laugh.
If he laughs well, he's a good man...."*
Fyodor Dostoyevsky

*"Whatever else an American believes or
disbelieves about himself, he is absolutely
sure he has a sense of humor."*
E.B. White

E.B. White was probably correct in saying that most of us *think* we have a good sense of humor. We like to think that we have the capacity to appreciate or understand not only jokes or comedy or funny stories but also the humor that occurs in everyday life. But I think that there are many people who never learn to see things in a humorous way. While they may chuckle at television sitcoms, funny movies, or professional comedians, they rarely appreciate the humor that happens all the time at home or the office, at the mall or the grocery store, with family members, colleagues, strangers, and friends.

Those professional comedians and comedy writers constantly look for the funny things that happen in everyday life. That's how they gather material. They observe and record what's going on around them. They look for humor everywhere – in the newspapers, at the gas station, in restaurants, in the neighborhood, at the office...yes, even on the freeways! And, as one professional humorist told me, they try to "think funny."

What a great way of looking at life! We could have more great days in our lives if we tried to see the humor in the ordinary and tried to "think funny." Doing this would certainly improve our attitudes and make us feel better about ourselves and the world around us. The Bible says that "a cheerful heart is good medicine," and we all can benefit from a generous dose of humor in our everyday lives.

I believe that one of the secrets of a happy marriage is a shared sense of humor. Humor and laughter in a relationship can keep problems in perspective, reduce boredom, and maintain a sense of intimacy and joy. One of the things I love most about my husband is that he makes me laugh. His wit and sense of fun enrich my life. In the book *Ties That Bind: How to Remain Happy as a Couple After the Wedding,* Victor Parachin says, "Unhappy couples are humorless couples. There is no joy in their lives. Couples that laugh together last together."

Several years ago our family had some very difficult financial problems. The loss of a job created stress and worry unlike any we had ever experienced. Our sons were teenagers, so they fully understood the challenges we were facing as a family. My husband and I shared everything with them, because we were all affected, and each family member was having to make sacrifices. One day the four of us were discussing our situation, and I must admit that my husband and I were feeling discouraged, depressed, and frightened. The situation was grave, and we didn't see any hope of immediate improvement. Our youngest son, Ben, who was 14 at the time, displayed wisdom beyond his years. He said, "Don't worry. Everything will be all right. All we need is faith and a sense of humor." He was absolutely right. That was exactly what we needed then and what all of us usually need to survive the tough times.

Today, pretend you're a comedy writer. Try to "think funny." Look for the funny things that happen at home, at work, and everywhere you go. Focus on the fun! When you start looking for it, you'll find it, and having a sense of humor will help you have great days.

38

Have Faith.

"Therefore, we do not lose heart. Though outwardly we are wasting away, yet inwardly we are being renewed day by day. For our light and momentary troubles are achieving for us an eternal glory that far outweighs them all. So we fix our eyes not on what is seen, but on what is unseen. For what is seen is temporary, but what is unseen is eternal."
2 Corinthians 4:16-18

"Now faith is being sure of what we hope for and certain of what we do not see."
Hebrews 11:1

Faith is an essential element in the lives of those people who consistently have great days. And it is the essential element that gives strength to those who are suffering. Our friend Jim Burns was an inspiration to all who knew him during the two years that he battled cancer. He always kept the faith. He never lost sight of the fact that God was in control of his life, and he never lost his sense of humor either. His favorite passage from the Bible, the one that sustained him and his family during their long months of pain, was the one above from 2 Corinthians 4:16-18.

Research indicates that religious people, those who have faith, are happier and more satisfied with life than nonbelievers, and there is impressive data which links religious faith with mental health. People who have faith are more optimistic about their present and their future. As Dr. David Myers puts it, "If I can believe that my long-term destiny is in God's loving hands, then I can cope with whatever awaits me from now till death."

There are many things in our lives over which we have no control. Both blessings and burdens will come to us, but a sure, consistent faith helps us keep both in perspective. Martin Luther wrote, "I've held many things in my hands and have lost them all. But all the things I've put in God's hands are still there."

39

Dream.

"You gotta have a dream.
If you don't have a dream,
How you gonna have a dream come true?"
Richard Rogers & Oscar Hammerstein

"All men dream...but not equally. They who
dream by night in the dusty recesses of their
minds wake up in the day to find that it is
vanity, but the dreamers of the day are
dangerous men, for they act their dreams
with open eyes and make it possible."
T.W. Lawrence

"To accomplish big things, I am convinced you
must first dream big dreams."
Conrad Hilton

"Dreams move on if you wait too long."
Billy Ray Cyrus

What are your dreams? Do you have some? I hope so. Dreams are the mental pictures of all those things that you would like to be, to have, to achieve, and dreamers have great days.

Scott Adams, creator of the popular "Dilbert" cartoon strip, had a rather meaningless job in a major corporation, the kind of job he now satirizes in his books and cartoons. Like Dilbert, Adams spent his work days buried in a cubicle at Pacific Bell's headquarters in northern California. During college, he wanted to be a cartoonist but was discouraged when he made the lowest grade in the one drawing course he took, so Adams opted for a degree in economics. But he didn't give up the dream. How did Scott Adams turn his dream into a reality? Read on...

40

Have Goals.

*"Don't let your short-term problems interfere
with your long-term goals."*
Ken Alexander

*"If you do not think about the future,
you cannot have one."*
John Galsworthy

*"If you don't know where you're going,
how can you expect to get there?"*
Basil S. Welsh

While dreams are often nebulous and not too clear, a goal is more focused, more definite, and therefore, more achievable. In her book, *Wishcraft,* Barbara Sher says, "It's easy to dream; with just a little encouragement you can close your eyes and conjure up a whole new life for yourself. But if you want to make that life come true, you will have to start by choosing one piece of it and deciding that that's the one you're going to go for first." And you've got to know what you want.

In the classic book *Alice in Wonderland,* Alice is walking along and comes to a fork in the road. She asks the Cheshire cat who is seated at the fork, "Which road should I take?" The Cheshire cat replies, "Where do you want to go?" Alice responds, "I don't know," to which the Cheshire cat says, "Then it doesn't matter which road you take."

Scott Adams knew which road he wanted to travel. He was very specific, and he began to affirm his goal. He began to write – "I will become a syndicated cartoonist" – 15 times a day. Every day he would write out his goal over and over and over again. He believed his goal to be a reality, and then he created a plan to make it happen.

All of us need goals, goals that are believable and achievable. Goals give us something to strive for and bring us a feeling of accomplishment and self-confidence. In Robert Frost's poem "Death of a Hired Man," the main characters, Warren and Mary, are discussing Silas, the hired man who has appeared at their farm after a long absence. Silas is old, sick, homeless, and has come to them hoping to be "taken in," though Mary suspects that he has come there to die. In talking about Silas and his life, Mary says that he had "...nothing to look backward to with pride, And nothing to look forward to with hope." We all need what Silas lacked. Having goals and working to accomplish them provides us with those necessary qualities of pride and hope.

Maybe you've never really thought about your dreams or your goals. Well, now is the time to start. Stop reading, and make a "wish list." Write down everything you'd like to do, to have, to accomplish in your life.

_____

_____

_____

_____

_____

_____

_____

_____

_____

_____

_____

_____

_____

_____

_____

_____

_____

Add more pages! List as many things as you can. Try for at least 50. Even if some of your wishes seem farfetched, write them down anyway.

Keep this list somewhere where you can refer to it often, and add other wishes as you think of them. There's magic just in the act of writing them down. Then pick one or two to work on first. Remember Scott Adams' technique? Write your goals 15 times each day. See yourself achieving your goal. And create a plan to make it happen.

What's on your "wish list"? Would you like to start a business, grow prize-winning tomatoes, run a marathon, write a book, build an canoe, sail around the world, attend a cooking school in Paris, volunteer your services to a charitable organization, get a pilot's license, spend more time with the ones you love, learn a foreign language? Write it down. You'll discover that the act of putting your wishes on paper begins the process of turning them into goals and making those goals real and attainable.

It's been said that success is the progressive realization of worthwhile goals. Those who enjoy great days spend their time and energy working toward a goal – something that helps them achieve their dreams, something of value, something that brings them pleasure, something that they can feel good about, something that provides a sense of pride and accomplishment. So dream a little...then decide on a goal, affirm it, establish a plan, and go for it!

41

Take Action.

*"Whatever you can do or dream you can,
begin it. Boldness has genius,
power and magic in it."*
Goethe

*"He slept beneath the moon,
He basked beneath the sun;
He lived a life of going-to-do
And died with nothing done."*
James Albery

*"Everyone who's ever taken a shower has
an idea. It's the person who gets out of the
shower, dries off and does something
about it who makes a difference."*
Nolan Bushnell

*"After all is said and done,
more is said than done."*
Unknown

*"The desire to do something
doesn't get it done."*
Unknown

"Make a move!"
Jack Whiteside

We all know that old adage which says that the road to you-know-where is paved with you-know-what. Nothing happens until we make it happen. So get busy. Do something. Take action...and have a great day!

42

Be Fun.

*"Let us so live that when we die
even the undertaker will be sad."*
Mark Twain

*"We don't stop having fun when we're old;
we're old when we stop having fun."*
Unknown

What a pleasure it is to be around people who are fun. They're the ones who smile, who are optimistic, who find humor even in difficult situations, and who make the time you spend with them enjoyable. They make you glad that you saw them. They help us have great days.

A wonderful story is told about Theodore Roosevelt. The day of his funeral, a ceremonial procession moved slowly and solemnly along Pennsylvania Avenue. Standing on a street corner was a policeman who, as the funeral procession passed by him, began to laugh. He was chuckling to himself.

The man standing next to him was shocked by his insensitive behavior. He couldn't believe the disrespect that the policeman was showing. In anger, he turned to the policeman and said, "How can you laugh at a time like this? How can you have such little respect for this great man? Surely you did not know him."

"On the contrary," said the policeman, "I knew him very well. I served with him during the Spanish-American War. We rode up San Juan Hill together, and I was just thinking that it was such fun being led by him."

Is that what your family or your co-workers would say about you? Is it fun being led by you? Is it fun working with you and for you?

When our youngest son, Ben, was about nine years old, the children in his Sunday school class made Thanksgiving place cards for their family members. These were to be used on the Thanksgiving table, and the children were to write on the place cards what they were thankful for with regard to each family member. I still have the place card that Ben made for me; I will treasure it always. On the outside, it said, "Mom," and on the inside it said, "Thanks for doing my clothes." (I liked that. It was a bit of appreciation.) And then he said, "Thanks for being fun."

I'm not always fun. I wish I could say that I am, but I'm not. Like most of us, I get tired and stressed and have too much to do and not enough time to do it. As my oldest son used to ask me, "Mom, are you pressed?" And I would say, "Honey, I'm ironed flat." I'm not always fun, but I'm trying, and I would encourage you to do the same.

When we're "fun," we add energy, enthusiasm, and enjoyment not only to our lives but also to the lives of those with whom we live and work. And maybe that's a small contribution we can make to helping this world be a better place.

43

Don't Wear Shoes That Hurt Your Feet.

If you do, it will <u>ruin</u> your day!

Great Days

44

Spend Time with Your Friends.

"Friendship is the sovereign antidote against all calamities."
Seneca

"Think where man's glory most begins and ends, and say my glory was I had such friends."
William Butler Yeats

"If one falls down, his friend can help him up. But pity the man who falls and has no one to help him up!"
Ecclesiastes 4:10

"I get by with a little help from my friends."
The Beatles

My life has been blessed with wonderful friends – those special people with whom I can laugh and cry, those precious human beings with whom I can share my heart, those cherished individuals who know me well and love me anyway. They truly make my days great ones.

There are the friends from childhood. It's amazing to think that friendships made so long ago can last so long. Certainly the years have changed us, but there are those special few with whom we "connected" back then who continue to impact us and to love us, those with whom we share lasting memories. They hold a special place in our hearts.

For my husband and me, there are our college friends who have remained so close through the years. What a unique privilege to have attended each other's weddings, watched our children grow up together, and then to come full circle and attend the weddings of our children. Friends like this are rare.

There are those couples whom we have known and loved through the years. Some we met in the early years of our marriage. In those days, we didn't have much money for going out or entertaining, but we had lots of fun-filled evenings of playing cards and eating popcorn. When we lived away from our families, we shared Thanksgiving dinners, and these special friends filled the lonely holes in our hearts.

There are the friends we met through our children, those Moms and Dads who served as extra pairs of eyes, watching out for our children just as we watched out for theirs.

There are those special families with whom we have traveled, camped, and skied. With them we've hugged the sides of mountains in 4-wheel drive Jeeps, white-knuckled with fear and awe-struck with the beauty. (On one of these trips our youngest son asked, "If we go over the side of this mountain, who gets our house?" Good question!) These couples and their children have become family, and we have a closeness that many blood relatives don't enjoy. There are the friends with whom we've shared the mountains, Jamaican sunsets, and New England foliage. All these have not only laughed with us and but also cried with us in hospital rooms and at funerals; we've shared the peaks and valleys of life.

There are my friends with whom I've enjoyed "girl" trips. We took Manhattan by a storm and came home with even more adventures than souvenirs.

And, of course, there are "the Babes," a unique group of eight warm, bright, funny women who celebrate birthdays together and who have shared so many joys and sorrows. Together we have laughed until we cried and cried until we had no tears left. Many things have changed our lives, but our friendship stays true.

There are my "speaker friends." I appreciate their support and encouragement. Unlike some others in my life, they truly understand what it is that I do for a living, and they understand, too, the perils and pleasures of our business.

There are my "church friends," a special fellowship of loving, caring individuals. We share similar beliefs and are supportive of each other in the good times and the bad.

How interesting and fun it is when one's children become adults and seem more like friends than offspring. Our sons continue to be a source of pride and delight. And how blessed I am to have a lovely daughter-in-law whose friendship is unique.

How can one have great days without the companionship, the caring, the fun of friendships? For me, the greatest days are those that are spent with my friends.

Take a Walk.

"Take two walks, and call me in the morning."
Unknown

"The only reason I would take up jogging is so that I could hear heavy breathing again."
Erma Bombeck

Walking is one of the best things you can do for yourself. It improves your health and lifts your spirits at the same time. Fitness experts rank walking as the #1 activity for most people. Old or young, fit or out of shape, walking is great for everyone. Even those who have never exercised regularly can benefit from a regular walking program. It requires no special skills, and you don't have to spend a lot of money on health club dues or expensive equipment. The only investment you need to make is in a good pair of walking shoes.

People who have established a regular walking program report weight loss, better sleep patterns, relief from stress and depression, improved self-confidence, better metabolism, elevated creativity, clearer thinking, increased energy, a more positive attitude...the list goes on and on. Walking at least 20 minutes each day will result in some positive changes; 20-60 minutes each day can change your life!

For best results, walk early in the morning. It will fire up your metabolism and mentally prepare you for the day ahead. If your schedule keeps you from walking then, just make sure you plan for it at some point during the day.

For me, walking makes me feel better, both mentally and physically. When I'm walking regularly, there is a positive difference in the way I feel and in my attitude. I like to set a weekly goal for myself and keep a record of how much I walk. Doing this keeps me on track and gives me a feeling of accomplishment.

What's the hardest part of getting started on a walking program? The hardest part is putting your shoes on and getting out the door. But if you can do that, you're on your way!

Give 100%.

*"For God's gift to you is more talent and ability
than you could ever use in one lifetime. Your gift
to God is to develop and utilize as much of that
talent and ability as you can in this lifetime."*
Bob Proctor

*"The differences between peak performers and
everybody else are much smaller
than 'everybody else' thinks."*
Charles Garfield

*"Life is like a 10-speed bicycle.
Most of us have gears we never use."*
Linus (Charles M. Schulz)

Have you ever tried to go swimming without getting your hair wet? Most of us have attempted this, usually without success. This futile effort often results in a) getting your hair at least damp and looking pretty bad anyway, b) not having much fun because you're so concerned about your hair, or c) all of the above.

In life's activities – whether it's in our work, our leisure, or our community projects – we are more productive and receive greater enjoyment if we just jump in, get "in the swim," and give those efforts 100%. To give

100% of our energy, our effort, our commitment to a project provides the greatest satisfaction and the greatest rewards.

In the 1996 Olympic games in Atlanta, a petite 18-year-old gymnast named Kerri Strug showed the world what it means to give 100%. Despite a painful injury to her ankle on the first attempt at the vault, Kerri made the decision to go for the second one anyway. Knowing that a second vault would worsen her already–injured ankle, Strug, in a rare demonstration of pure courage, went all out to help win the first-ever gold medal for the U.S. women's gymnastic team.

The next day *USA Today* said that Kerri's vault "ranks near the top of any list of great sporting moments." The newspaper went on to say, "Our sports need players like Strug. Our kids need role models like Strug. Our society needs moments like hers." When people give 100%, they become an inspiration to others. Richard E. Byrd, an early polar explorer and the first person to fly over the North Pole, said, "Few men during their lifetime come anywhere near exhausting the resources dwelling within them. There are deep wells of strength that are never used."

Unlike Kerri Strug or Richard Byrd, most of us will never be in a position that forces us to go all out; most of us will not be asked to make that kind of sacrifice. But all of us have the opportunity each day to give 100% – to do our best at whatever it is we do.

So, today – whatever it is that you will be doing – give it your best. In everything you do, tell yourself that "good enough" is not good enough. Whether you're making a sales call, baking cookies, chairing a committee, writing a report, repairing a car, teaching a class – jump in head first. Give it 100%...and have a great day.

47

Enjoy the Little Things.

*"Life is a banquet, darling, and most poor
people are starving to death."*
Auntie Mame

*"I'd rather have roses on my table
than diamonds on my neck."*
Emma Goldman

*"Without ice cream, there would be
chaos and darkness."*
Don Kardong

Those people who enjoy life to its fullest are those who find pleasure and delight in the little things. They're the ones who pay attention to the details, who delight in the moment, who allow their senses to relish the infinite variety of life. The world offers us so many simple pleasures, but we rarely take time to notice.

To have great days, pay attention to the little things. Enjoy the beauty of fresh vegetables in the supermarket, the texture of fabric, the warmth of the sun, the feel of cool grass on bare feet, the smell of fresh baked bread, the sound of a gentle rain, the sweet sensation of a chocolate kiss...or a real one.

Delight in the sound of a child's laughter, the cozy warmth of a fire, the gentle touch of the breeze on your face, the fragrance of a flower, the sighting of a cardinal, the comfort of a hug. Appreciate a cool drink of water, a warm bed, the sound of rustling leaves, the beauty of a sunset, the humbling sight of the night sky, the aroma of cookies warm from the oven.

Relish the taste of ice cream, the enthusiasm of a puppy, the softness of a baby's skin, the pleasure of a shower or a bubble bath, the delight of a quiet moment spent with someone you love.

Pleasures abound for those who look for them. We find what we seek, and if we seek beauty and joy in the little things, we will find more than what we expected.

48

Count Your Blessings.

"When upon life's billows
you are tempest-tossed,
When you are discouraged,
thinking all is lost,
Count your many blessings,
name them one by one,
And it will surprise you
what the Lord hath done.
Count your blessings,
Name them one by one;
Count your blessings,
See what God hath done;
Count your blessings,
Name them one by one;
Count your many blessings,
See what Got hath done."
Hymn by E.O. Excell

While all our days may not be great ones, each of us is the recipient of innumerable blessings. Make a list of your blessings...and have a great day.

1. _____

2. _____

3. _____

4. _____

5. _____

6. _____

7. _____

8. _____

9. _____

10. _____

11. _____

12. _____

13. _____

14. _____

15. _____

16. _____

Add more pages!

49

Learn to Bounce Back.

*"It's not whether you get knocked down.
It's whether you get up again."*
Vince Lombardi

*"Life is full of unexpected hurdles.
The rules are – you can't go around them or knock
them down; just clear them and land safely."*
Lou Beth Birdwell

*"Success isn't permanent,
and failure isn't fatal."*
Mike Ditka

"Fall seven times, stand up eight."
Japanese Proverb

When our boys were growing up, they had a bop bag. This inflatable toy was weighted in the bottom. It looked like Batman or Superman and was designed in such a way that when it was hit, it would fall over but then would bounce back up again.

There are lessons to be learned from the bop bag. Life is going to knock us down, but just because we're knocked down doesn't mean we have to stay down. Like the bop bag, we can bounce back up again.

We human beings have amazing resiliency and more courage and determination than we can ever imagine. Learn a lesson from the bop bag super heroes. When life knocks you down, bounce back.

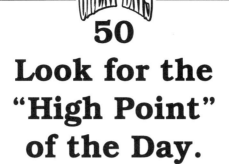

50

Look for the "High Point" of the Day.

*"No matter how hard the winter,
spring always comes."*
Unknown

"'Tis always morning somewhere in the world."
Richard Henry Hengist Horne

"Every cloud has a silver lining."
Unknown

*"There are no bad days.
Some are just better than others."*
Bob Murphey

There's bad news, and there's good news. The bad news is that, in spite of our best efforts, not every day will be a great one. But you already know that, don't you? You already know that in spite of an optimistic attitude, positive partners, music, smiles, prayer, friends, faith, and even chocolate, you're going to have some bad days along the way. That's the reality of life.

The good news is that even bad days have moments that are better than others. And we have to find comfort in that.

A woman told me a story about her aunt that I think contains a lesson for all of us. Her aunt was in her nineties when she died, and when the family was sorting through her things, they found a journal that she had kept the last few years of her life. In those last years she lived alone, and her poor health caused her to have a somewhat confined and lonely existence. And yet at the end of each day's entry in her journal, she had written "high point of the day."

For her, the "high point" was sometimes a call from a friend or a visit from a neighbor. There were days when someone from the church had dropped in with homemade soup or muffins and others when the "high point" was that her arthritis was less painful than it was the day before. Sometimes it was a card from a friend, a letter or phone call from a distant relative, or the sight of a cardinal in her backyard.

The message here is that every day, even in her limited world, she found a "high point."

Let me encourage you to look for the "high point" of the day. Instead of focusing on the negatives, look for the positives – the things you're grateful for, the many blessings that you've received, the little things that add joy to life. Not every day is going to be a great one, but even the bad days have some small moment that is an expression of joy or hope or love if we only look for it.

Look for the "high point" of each day, and think about how your presence, your attitude, your smile, your laughter, your kindness can become a "high point" for someone else.

As Annie Dillard said, "How we spend our days is how we spend our lives." Let's choose to make each day an investment and to spend our days in ways that add energy, enthusiasm, and enjoyment to our lives and the lives of others.

Have a great day.

Order Form

To order additional autographed copies of **Great Days! 50 Ways to Add Energy, Enthusiasm, & Enjoyment to Your Life**, please send $11.95 per copy plus $2.55 shipping and handling.

Enclosed is my check for _____ made payable to **Great Days Presentations** for _____ copies.

Name _____

Address _____

City _____ State ___ Zip ____

If you would like a personalized inscription on gift copies, please include the name of each recipient with your order.

Great Days Presentations
2002 Shari Lane
Garland, TX 75043